TO LOVE IS TO FLY

# TO LOVE IS TO FLY

### Images by Jonathan Chester

### Words by Patrick Regan

**Andrews McMeel
Publishing, LLC**

Kansas City · Sydney · London

09 10 11 12 13 SDB 10 9 8 7 6 5 4 3 2

ISBN-13: 978-0-7407-8510-8
ISBN-10: 0-7407-8510-9

Library of Congress Control Number: 2009922404

www.andrewsmcmeel.com

ATTENTION: SCHOOLS AND BUSINESSES
Andrews McMeel books are available at quantity discounts with bulk purchase for educational, business, or sales promotional use. For information, please write to: Special Sales Department, Andrews McMeel Publishing, LLC, 1130 Walnut Street, Kansas City, Missouri 64106.

Most mysteries
    of the universe
have already been
    explained.

We know
   that gravity
   makes things
   drop.

We have a pretty good idea
why the wind blows.

We even know why
some birds can fly
and some cannot.

But there's still one mystery that defies easy explanation.

What makes otherwise
perfectly normal folks
fall hopelessly,
helplessly
in love?

Ah, yes . . . love . . .
that sublime emotion,
that unexplainable
phenomenon that
sends an electric charge
through heart, brain,
stomach, and various
other body parts.

How does it happen? Why does it hit some harder than others? There are plenty of experts, but does anyone really know?

In the endless sea of
wandering souls, how

16

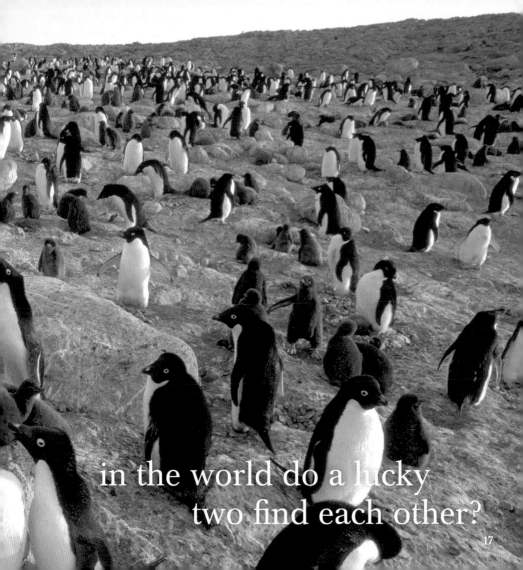

in the world do a lucky
two find each other?

17

Sometimes
the attraction is immediate
and mutual . . .

. . . the pace of love
frenzied and feverish.

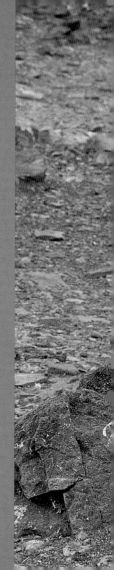

(This is exhilarating,
but can, of course,
leave those involved
completely exhausted.)

23

More likely, love begins with a spark—a moment of mutual captivation and innocent recognition of shared interest.

Things often begin slowly.

27

A stolen
glance
becomes a
flirtatious
gaze.

There are advances . . .

. . . and retreats.

Moments of
hope and glory . . .

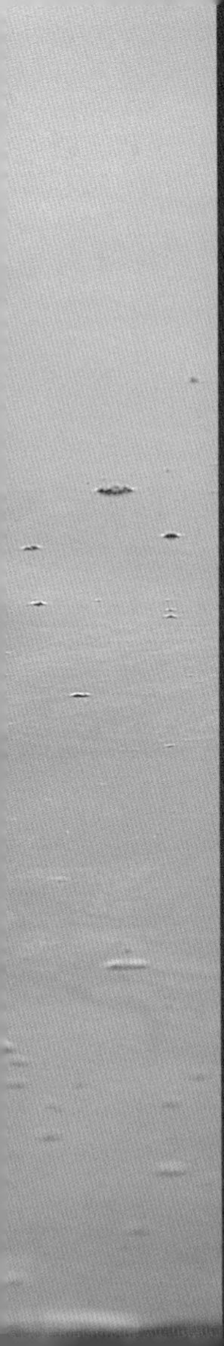

. . . are followed
by periods of
disappointment
and despair.

A timeless dance
has begun.

Suddenly, we're looking
for any excuse to
spend time with
each other.

We try to separate from the pack as often as possible.

Before giving in completely to
the power of our emotions,

we often stop to check ourselves
and the strength of our heart.

We confer with trusted friends to make sure they don't see warning signs we've somehow missed in the blinding fog of attraction.

If their advice runs contrary to our emotions, we do the wise thing—ignore it.

49

Such is the
determination of
the fool in love.

We find that the object
of our affection is quite
unlike any other.

The more we know,
the more we like.

We search our souls,
and find that there's no
use denying it . . .

This is the real thing.

The Big One.

This is love!

And suddenly
everything has
changed.

From this day on,
there are adventures
to undertake,

challenges to
face together,

and secret dreams to share.

The future, which at
times seemed empty
and featureless,

now holds all kinds
of possibilities.
(Some a little frightening.)

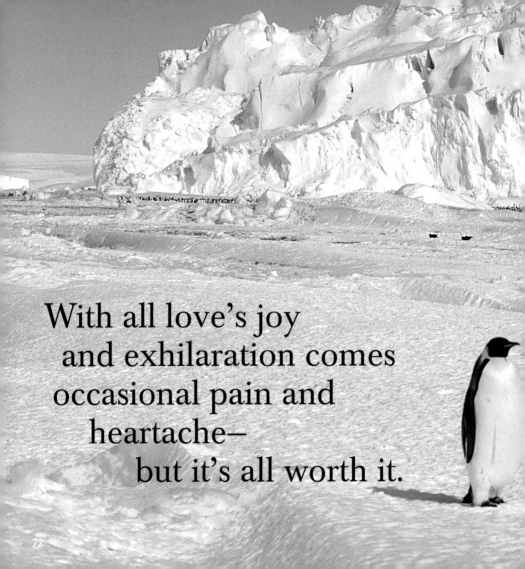

With all love's joy
and exhilaration comes
occasional pain and
heartache—
but it's all worth it.

Because love also brings the comforting knowledge that we will always have a shoulder to lean on and a warm body to cuddle on a cold, winter night.

And that even on days
when we may not look our best,

our loved one sees the best in us.

Real love is unconditional,
unending, unequivocal, un . . .

unlike anything else.

Real love is
discovering for
the first time that
we truly can fly.

Believe me, I know.

And it's all
because
of you.

# IMAGE KEY

**Front Cover**
King penguins
*Aptenodytes patagonica*
Volunteer Point, Falkland Islands
Kings can stand still for many minutes
beak-to-beak in the stateliest of mating rituals. They conduct an elaborate
courtship involving antiphonal (alter-
nating response) duets, advertisement
walks, and lots of bowing.

**Page ii**
King penguins
Macquarie Island, Australia
In the daytime, king penguins may
dive as deep as 1,150 feet (350 me-
ters) for a duration exceeding seven
minutes in search of their typical
prey, the lanternfish. At night, the
lanternfish are closer to the surface
so their dives are shallower.

**Page v**
King penguins
Gold Harbor, South Georgia
King penguins are predominately a
sub-Antarctic species. Some of the
largest concentrations of kings are
on South Georgia, home to over
400,000 breeding pairs.

**Page 1**
Gentoo penguins
*Pygoscelis papua*
Falkland Islands
Gentoos tend to occupy colonies on
low, open coastal plains in the sub-
Antarctic. They live year-round on
the Falkland Islands but occasionally
the entire colony relocates several
hundred yards in search of cleaner
surroundings.

**Page 3**
Adélie penguins
*Pygoscelis adelie*
Davis Station, Antarctica
Adélies often gather on an ice edge
where they wait for the opportune
moment to dive in en masse to
reduce the danger of being eaten by
patrolling leopard seals.

**Page 4**
Adélie penguins
Commonwealth Bay, Antarctica
This true Antarctic species is at
home in the coldest of conditions,
such as the high winds and blowing
snow that occur during a "ground"
blizzard.

**Page 7**
Adélie penguins
Davis Station, Antarctica
The only predator on land for
Antarctic penguins is the skua. These
aerial pirates often work in tandem
to steal eggs and attack chicks or
injured adults. A healthy adult can
usually fend them off, however.

**Page 8**
Antarctic Peninsula
Grounded icebergs are carved by the
water and waves as the tide rises and
falls. As light penetrates deeper into
solid ice, more and more of the red
wavelengths are absorbed, thus the
reflected light appears very blue.

**Page 10**
Gentoo penguins
Falkland Islands
In the sub-Antarctic, gentoos begin breeding in late September, the austral (southern) spring, which usually results in two eggs being laid in late October.

**Page 18**
Adélie penguins
Commonwealth Bay, Antarctica
Penguin pairs will often point to the sky and call back and forth in a cackling trill. This is known as mutual trumpeting, which is integral to the pair-bonding process.

**Page 13**
Adélie penguin
Commonwealth Bay, Antarctica
The Adélie has dense feathers to the very tip of its bill, one of the many adaptations that give it the ability to survive in extreme conditions.

**Page 21**
Adélie penguins
Commonwealth Bay, Antarctica
In the lead-up to mating, the male Adélie spreads out his pile of pebbles with his bill and invites the female to lie on this rudimentary nest. The following copulation is quite a balancing act.

**Page 15**
King penguins
South Georgia
The king penguin's pronounced yellow-colored ear patch is very vibrant in breeding adults. Males show this off by head flagging (pronounced waving back and forth) as they perform their advertisement walk to a prospective mate.

**Page 23**
Chinstrap penguins
*Pygoscelis antarctica*
Hanna Point, South Shetland Islands
Penguins often sleep lying down, usually on the ground rather than a rocky perch. This pair is in the process of fledging; they are losing their down feathers and developing adult plumage.

**Page 16**
Adélie penguins
Davis Station, Antarctica
Adélies like to call loudly to their mates as they enter and leave the rookery (and many other times as well). When an entire colony takes up the call in unison, it can be very raucous.

**Page 24**
King penguins
Volunteer Point, Falkland Islands
This is the most northerly and easily accessible breeding colony of king penguins in the world. It is a four-hour overland drive from Stanley, which has air service from South America.

Page 26
Chinstrap penguins
Bailey Head, Deception Island
Chinstrap penguins are a very
gregarious species and their colonies
can be extremely large. They
typically develop strong bonds,
pairing up with the same mate from
one year to the next.

Page 34
Gentoo penguins
Petermann Island,
Antarctic Peninsula
This ecstatic display is common
to all three brush-tailed penguin
species, indicating its central role
and importance in pair bonding and
courtship.

Page 28
King penguins
St. Andrews Bay, South Georgia
King penguins are the most
colorful and arguably the most
beautiful species, but they were also
heavily exploited for their oil in
the nineteenth and early twentieth
centuries.

Page 36
Gentoo penguins
Antarctic Peninsula
The transition from the land to
the water is an awkward time for
penguins as they are vulnerable to
predation from leopard seals. They
usually make the speediest entry
possible.

Page 30
King penguins
Gold Harbor, South Georgia
Kings are serially monogamous,
having only one mate each year.
But in successive years, pairs only
stay together 30 percent of the time.
This is possibly a function of their
long breeding cycle, which is some
fourteen to sixteen months.

Page 39
King penguins
Volunteer Point, Falkland Islands
The king penguin's mating ritual
includes the advertisement walk, an
exaggerated waddling gait where
the head makes a pendulum motion.
The male usually leads off, followed
in unison by the female.

Page 32
King penguins
South Georgia
King penguins have a peculiar
stance; they are able to balance on
the back of their heels for hours on
end. This adaptation for conserving
heat is especially valuable when
they are incubating an egg on top of
their feet.

Page 41
King penguins
Volunteer Point, Falkland Islands
Kings are especially strong
swimmers and deep divers.
Immature and nonbreeding birds
disperse and travel long distances
from land.

**Page 42**
Adélie penguins
Brown Bluff, Antarctic Peninsula
Penguins live most of their lives at sea, but the true Antarctic species often rest or sleep on floating ice that, if large enough, gives them some protection from predators.

**Page 44**
Gentoo penguins
Falkland Islands
The total population of gentoo penguins is around 315,000. Colonies on the Antarctica Peninsula are increasing. However, in the sub-Antarctic, numbers are declining sufficiently enough to earn the gentoo the status of "near threatened" on the International Union for Conservation of Nature (IUCN) Red List.

**Page 46**
Magellanic penguins
*Spheniscus magellanicus*
Falkland Islands
Magellanic penguins are members of the so-called "ringed penguin" group. All of the four ringed species have a semicircular-shape white feather pattern on their heads.

**Page 48**
King penguins
Salisbury Plain, South Georgia
Although much of a king penguin's life ashore is spent in close proximity to other kings, the adults do not form a "turtle" (huddle) like emperor penguins do in the face of extreme cold.

**Page 50**
Gentoo penguins
Falkland Islands
Gentoos walk into the water until their flippers are half covered, then they swim submerged a short distance before coming to the surface to wash themselves.

**Page 53**
Adélie penguin (L)
Emperor penguin (R), *Aptenodytes forsteri*
Auster Rookery, Mawson Station, East Antarctica
Adélie and emperor penguins are both true Antarctic species that breed on the Antarctic continent.

**Page 54**
Gentoo penguins
Falkland Islands
Unlike Adélie and chinstrap penguins, gentoos can be quite wary of humans in some locations and so should not be approached too closely.

**Page 56**
Adélie penguin
Antarctic Peninsula
Well adapted to surviving in cold conditions on land or at sea, penguins can easily overheat when it is warm. To cool off, they stand with outstretched flippers and let the blood dissipate the heat.

**Page 58**
King penguins
Gold Harbor, South Georgia
Kings are unique among penguin species because their breeding cycle requires more than one year to raise a chick.

**Page 61**
Chinstrap penguins
Antarctic Peninsula
Almost all penguin species "porpoise" when traveling long distances, as this is their most effective mode of transportation. They are able to breathe as they leap in and out of the water while also maintaining laminar flow over their plumage.

**Page 63**
King penguins
Volunteer Point, Falkland Islands
As part of their courting ritual, king penguins do a little two-step waddling walk, one behind the other. This is followed by mutual display and then copulation.

**Page 64**
Gentoo penguins
Neko Harbor, Antarctic Peninsula
Gentoo pairs are loyal to each other and reunite year after year. Unlike Adélie and chinstrap penguins, they disperse on the peninsula but do not migrate, which further enhances their ability to maintain pair bonds.

**Page 66**
King penguins
St. Andrews Bay, South Georgia
King penguins often stand onshore in or by a shallow stream, which gives them a ready supply of drinking water. This is especially valuable for the two to three weeks when they are molting and need to conserve their energy.

**Page 68**
Emperor penguins
Auster Rookery, East Antarctica
The sea in deep Antarctica freezes solid to a depth of several feet, which forces these birds to make long treks to get to their breeding areas, usually in proximity to grounded icebergs

**Page 70**
Emperor penguins
Auster Rookery, East Antarctica
Each emperor penguin pair can have just one chick each breeding season, but they raise their young in close proximity to the colony for protection from the cold and predators.

**Page 72**
Emperor penguins
Auster Rookery, East Antarctica
Emperor penguins breed in winter in Antarctica and as a result they often have to travel long distances over the frozen sea ice to get to their feeding grounds.

**Page 75**
King penguins
St. Andrews Bay, South Georgia
Pair formation is a drawn-out
business for king penguins. Males
perform the so-called "ecstatic
display," then pairs call back and
forth to each other. Pair forming also
includes lots of bowing and head
flagging by the males.

**Page 82**
King penguins
Gold Harbor, South Georgia
King penguins are predominately a
sub-Antarctic species, and some of
the largest concentrations of kings
are on South Georgia.

**Page 76**
King penguins
South Georgia
Depending on the colony, at
between forty to sixty weeks of age,
king chicks shed their furry down
for a coat resembling adult plumage.
This process, known as fledging,
leaves them looking very disheveled.

**Page 84**
King penguins
Volunteer Point, Falkland Islands
Courting kings can stand still for
many minutes beak-to-beak in the
stateliest of mating rituals.

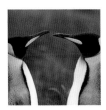

**Page 78**
King penguins
Volunteer Point, Falkland Islands
The dramatic orange ear patch on
the king is much brighter than on the
slightly larger emperor penguin.

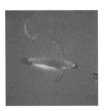

**Page 80**
King penguins
Macquarie Island, Australia
Penguins are completely at home
in the sea, diving to great depths as
they hunt for prey. They literally
"fly" underwater, using their flippers
to propel themselves, albeit in a
denser medium than air.

# Penguins Need Love, Too

It is very easy to fall in love with penguins, especially if you are lucky enough to encounter them in the wild. Even if you only meet them in a zoo or an aquarium, they can quickly win your heart. Furthermore, their inimitable appeal is revealed in their warm depictions in films, photos, and cartoons. In their native realm, however, most of the world's penguins are far removed from human interaction; thus, it is very hard to keep track of how they are surviving. In the face of unprecedented threats from overfishing, habitat destruction, oil spills, and the biggest threat of all, global warming, there is much to be concerned about.

Dedicated scientists are currently studying penguins and monitoring their well-being, including the species that live in deep Antarctica, such as the Adélie penguin and the extraordinary emperor penguin. Using sophisticated new technologies, we are learning a good deal about their current condition. Radio-frequency identification tags—the same microchip devices replacing bar codes in retail stores and being used to recover lost pets—are injected into penguins so that they can be remotely identified and monitored as they cross a weighbridge entering and leaving a breeding colony. Satellites, which are being used to track small data loggers and transmitters that have been glued onto penguins' backs, are becoming valuable tools as well. Some of the larger species are now even wearing miniature video cameras and time-depth recorders when they dive into the inky depths to hunt for food.

Through this work, we are learning that Antarctic species are being significantly affected by anthropogenic warming. We have known for some time that the Antarctic Peninsula is warming at two to three times the global average, and that since 1978 the average time per year the ocean around the Antarctic Peninsula is covered by sea ice has fallen by ninety days. The latest research resulting from the recently concluded Fourth International Polar Year indicates that global warming is also changing the chemistry of the Southern Ocean, with air pollution making it more acidic and the melting ice lowering its salinity. All these factors are dramatically affecting the web of life in Antarctica, which is so closely tied to the survival of the krill, the tiny shrimplike crustacean that is in turn dependent on the sea ice.

Global warming is affecting the distribution of penguins in very specific ways. With the peninsula climate becoming more sub-Antarctic, Adélie penguins are being pushed farther south, and chinstraps and gentoos are replacing them. In the Ross Sea, Adélies are now more successful in places because the warming ocean gives them easier access to their breeding grounds. But the concern is that they could eventually run out of room to relocate themselves. The northernmost emperor colonies are in decline as well because the thinner sea ice blows away before the chicks are sufficiently large to survive at sea.

Farther north, king penguins (as seen on the cover) are not exempt from stress, either. Long-term studies show that populations are declining in certain colonies as the sea temperatures warm and the king penguins have to swim farther and farther to find adequate fish supplies. When king penguins are away from home for long periods of time, their chicks are fed less frequently and their breeding success is reduced.

Wildlife Conservation Society biologist P. Dee Boersma has been studying Magellanic penguins in Argentina for twenty-five years. Recently dubbed the Jane Goodall of penguins, she has documented a 22 percent decline in the Punto Tombo colony since 1987. This and other similar reports of declines across the Southern Hemisphere have resulted in the IUCN giving the Magellanic and eleven other species out of a total of seventeen species of penguins, the status of "near threatened." Changes in the availability and abundance of prey due to both climate change and exploitation of the Magellanic's food sources by overfishing are at the root of its problems.

P. Dee Boersma's Penguin Project and many other similar efforts by scientists and nonprofit organizations can benefit greatly from your concern and interest. Field research in such far-off places is challenging and expensive. You can show penguins more than a little love by donating to or supporting one of the following organizations:

### THE PENGUIN PROJECT
**http://mesh.biology.washington.edu/penguinProject/home**

### PENGUIN SCIENCE
**http://www.penguinscience.com**

### ANTARCTIC AND SOUTHERN OCEAN COALITION (ASOC)
**http://www.krillcount.org/**

### OCEANITIES
**http://www.oceanites.org/**

–JONATHAN CHESTER